TINY TRUTHS
JOURNAL FOR LIVING A BIG LIFE

Accompaniment to the book
Ten Tiny Truths,
Principles for Living a Big Life
by Erin Anderson.

TINY TRUTHS JOURNAL

Copyright © 2020 Erin Anderson, Live Big Co.

All rights reserved. No part of this publication may be reproduced, distributed, or transmitted in any form or by any means, including photocopying, recording, digital scanning, or other electronic or mechanical methods, without the prior written permission of the publisher, except in the case of brief quotations embodied in critical reviews and certain other uses permitted by copy-write law. For permission requests, please contact hello@livebigco.com.

Cover design by Erin Anderson
Book design by Erin Anderson

Contact the author: www.livebigco.com

Soft cover ISBN: 978-1-7774592-1-5

First printing 2021

Be messy, and complicated, and afraid
and show up anyways.

- GLENNON DOYLE

NOTHING BUT THE TRUTH

So much of our lives are documented, shared and liked, or not. We have fewer and fewer private moments and this life on display has caused stress to many of us. So much so that the self-care movement became monumental.

The stress of keeping up, looking good and keeping it together can crush our sensitive soul. Unless we don't let that happen.

How we as humans process our emotions is as unique as our finger prints. There is no one way to move the energy of feelings, thoughts and ideas through our bodies. There is no correct or magical way to convert our life experiences into wisdom. But from years of experiencing challenges, trauma, joy, loss, pain, success, failures and egg on my face I've learned that writing is the most effective way to get to the truth of the matter.

Writing with a pen, not a keyboard, has a way of drawing out the truth. The ink in your pen is a magical elixir that only delivers the truth, the whole truth and nothing but the truth.

Use these pages to explain the unexplainable, to examine the unexamined, to let lose that which has been trapped within.

This is your book, not to be shared or divided up. There is no algorithm, no likes, no comments from the outside world. This is your heart, mind and soul poured out onto these pages for your higher self to be set free.

And really, let your lowest form have a voice here. Let your messy middle pour out and let it be.

I wrote the book *Ten Tiny Truths, Principles for Living a Big Life* as a way to share principles that have helped me move through my life with the truth at my side. As a coach helping people tune into their purpose so they can make an authentic contribution, the principles I learned from my late mum have been invaluable. I have become aware of each one as I bumped up against my blocks or as I celebrated my success.

This journal will serve you on it's own or as a companion to the book.

Reflecting on the questions, writing and drawing, is productive work. When you get close to your true voice you tap into your power. Our inner saboteur doesn't like this work. The saboteur wants to lie to you and tell you it's not worth it. The reality is, truth and lies cannot co-exist.

Enjoy the adventure of discovery and true self-awareness. With joy and love you will tap into the truth of your inner power and open the doors of possibility.

The truth is a gift that exceeds all other gifts.

When it's over, I want to say:
all my life I was a bride
married to amazement.
I was the bridegroom, taking
the world into my arms.

- MARY OLIVER

YOU ARE THE AUTHOR

You get to create your life. If this idea doesn't come easily, this is the place to work out what gets in the way of it. If you do believe that you are always in choice and the author of your life then this is the place to get in touch with your authority on a deeper level.

Being the author of your life means you get to shape the experience you are having. This doesn't mean you get to take a pass when tough times head your way. It does mean that you can choose your response and the meaning you place on the events that happen no matter how wonderful or brutal.

Use these pages to work out the comedy, drama, horror or reality show that is your life.

I'll provide you with some inspiration and journal prompts to get things flowing.

You may notice that this journal has no lines. You get to let your thoughts and ideas roam free!

Let your answers pour out of you so you can live your big beautiful life in the flow of creation.

THE ADVENTURE BEGINS

YOU HAVE A SONG TO SING
Know what lights you up and do more of it.

90% OF LIFE IS SHOWING UP
Showing up is undervalued. You showing up makes all the difference.

RISE TO THE OCCASION
Life asks big questions, you rise up and answer.

DON'T TRY HARD, GET REAL
Authenticity is a super power.

BE A FOUNTAIN NOT A DRAIN
Giving and receiving is fulfilling, any other result is a drain.

PERFECT IS BORING
What you look like never trumps how you feel.

CONTRIBUTION HAPPENS IN THE NOW
Here and now is all we have.

YOU ARE ALWAYS INFLUENCING
More people are listening to you than you think.

FORGIVE TO LIVE BIG
Your big life is on the other side of forgiveness.

TINY JOYS CREATE A BIG LIFE
God is in the details.

YOU HAVE A SONG TO SING

Don't die with your music still inside you.

- DR. WAYNE DYER

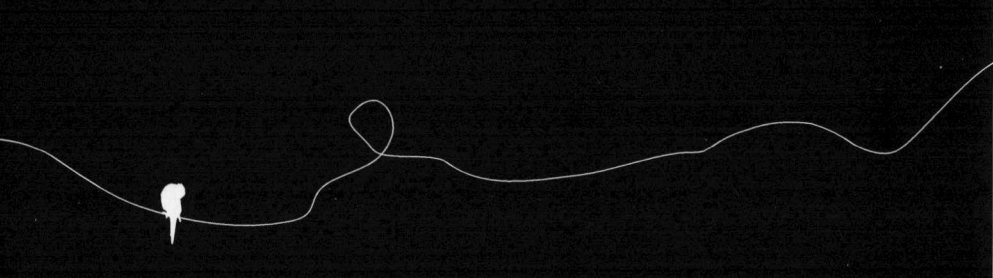

THINGS I'M PROUD OF MY SELF FOR

THINGS I'M PROUD OF MYSELF FOR THAT
NOBODY KNOWS ABOUT

AWE TO ME IS...

THAT'S MY JAM

What are your top 10 songs that make your soul move. Doodle or colour in an icon.

1 ☐ _____
BY _____

2 ☐ _____
BY _____

3 ☐ _____
BY _____

4 ☐ _____
BY _____

5 ☐ _____
BY _____

6 ☐ _____
BY _____

7 ☐ _____
BY _____

8 ☐ _____
BY _____

9 ☐ _____
BY _____

10 ☐ _____
BY _____

IN MY LIFE I HOPE TO...

THERE'S A STAGE YOU'RE BEING CALLED UP TO. DESCRIBE WHAT FOR?

WHAT I MOST WANT TO BE KNOWN FOR IN MY LIFETIME...

THAT'S SO ME

Circle the thing that fits who you are at your core.

Metallica *Joni Mitchell*

Lipstick *Chapstick*

Yoga *Weights*

Fast *Slow*

Audible *Books*

Magazine *Pinterest*

Camping *Hotel*

Beach *Mountain*

Abstract *Precision*

Tidy *Lived in*

Salsa *Hip Hop*

Extrovert *Introvert*

Last minute *Prepared*

IF YOU WERE TO GET A TATTOO, WHAT WOULD IT BE? DRAW OR DOODLE IT.

**90% OF LIFE
IS SHOWING UP**

My mission in life is not merely to survive,
but to thrive; and to do so with some
passion, some compassion, some
humour, and some style.

- MAYA ANGELOU

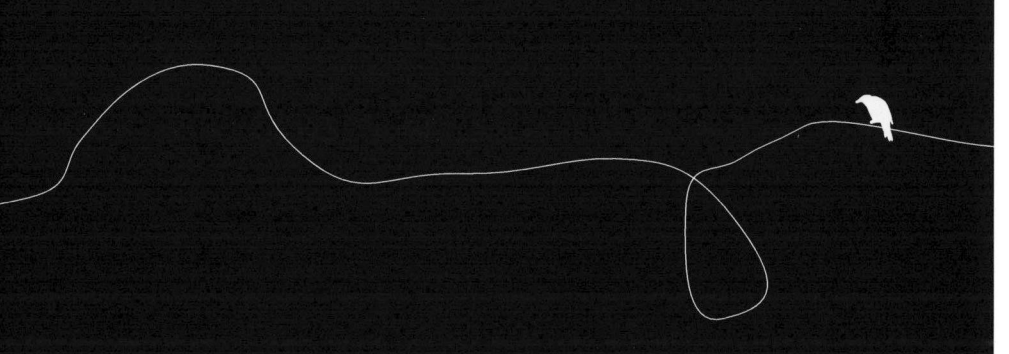

WHAT'S THE BOOK YOU WISH SOMEONE WOULD WRITE?

WRITE THE OUTLINE.

SUCCESS TO ME IS...

WHAT DO YOU DROOL OVER, OBSESS ABOUT,
THINK ABOUT ALL THE TIME?

WHO IS YOUR 3AM PERSON AND WHY? WHEN THEY CALL, YOU SHOW UP.

WHAT GETS YOUR HELL YES?

**DON'T TRY HARD,
GET REAL**

I don't want to be remembered as the girl
who was shot, I want to be remembered
as the girl who stood up.

- MALALA YOUSAFZAI

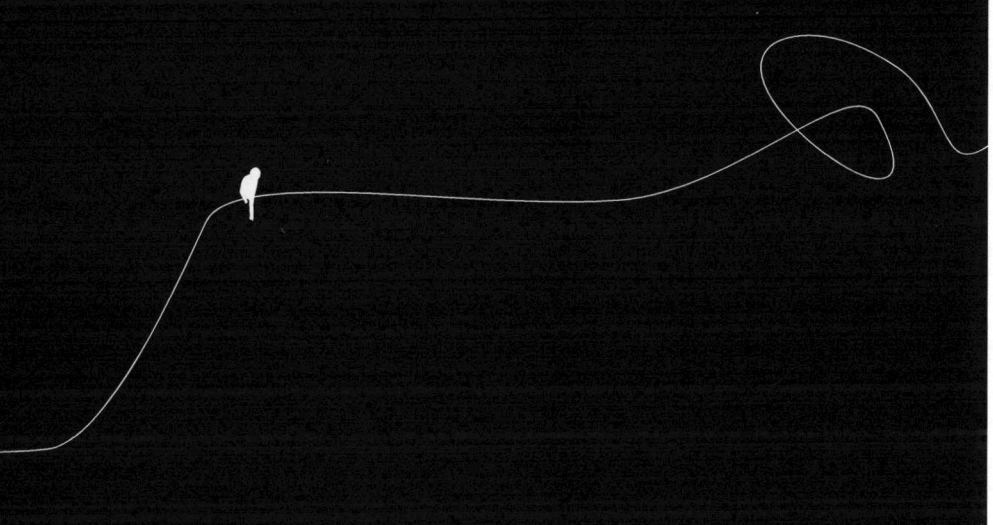

WHERE DO YOU FEEL MOST ALIVE AND FULLY YOURSELF? WHAT ARE YOU DOING, WHO ARE YOU WITH?

HOW DO YOU ACT OR SOUND LIKE WHEN YOU FEEL INAUTHENTIC?

HOW DO YOU FEEL WHEN YOU'RE AROUND PEOPLE WHO SEEM FAKE?

WHAT ARE THE MOST GENUINE ATTRIBUTES ABOUT YOU?

Check all that apply and add more!

- [ ] *kind*
- [ ] *inspired*
- [ ] *generous*
- [ ] *spontaneous*
- [ ] *conscientious*
- [ ] *collaborative*
- [ ] *flexible*
- [ ] *accurate*
- [ ] *motivated*
- [ ] *elegant*
- [ ] *sensual*

- [ ] *funny*
- [ ] *emotional*
- [ ] *thoughtful*
- [ ] *pensive*
- [ ] *generative*
- [ ] *determined*
- [ ] *helpful*
- [ ] *creative*
- [ ] *cautious*
- [ ] *bold*
- [ ] *optimistic*

USE THIS PAGE TO DOODLE, WRITE, COLOUR OR DRAW HOW YOU MOST WANT TO FEEL.

INTERVIEW YOUR PEOPLE. ASK 3 - 5 PEOPLE WHO SUPPORT YOU THESE QUESTIONS:

What do you most admire or appreciate about me?

When do you notice I shrink?

When do you notice I shine?

What attribute about me do you believe I can highlight more?

What outcomes do you most want for me?

What do you believe my purpose in life is?

INSIGHTS FROM THE EXERCISE.

**BE A FOUNTAIN
NOT A DRAIN**

Negative thinking is something we all do.
The difference between the person who is primarily
optimistic and the person who is primarily pessimistic
is that the optimist learns to become a good debater.
Once you become thoroughly aware of the effectiveness
of optimism in your life, you can learn to
debate your pessimistic thoughts.

— STEVE CHANDLER

WHEN DO YOU FEEL FULFILLED?

WHAT DRAINS YOU?

WHAT DO YOU VALUE? CIRCLE ALL THE VALUES THAT FEEL LIKE YOU, AND ADD NEW ONES!

authenticity	*truth*	*purposefulness*
harmony	*honour*	*finesse*
rigor	*creativity*	*fun*
love	*connection*	*clarity*
joy	*tolerance*	*charisma*
contribution	*justice*	*beauty*
precision	*equanimity*	*wisdom*
integrity	*growth*	*peace*
choice	*patience*	*joy*
acceptance	*faith*	*humour*
flow	*change*	*forgiveness*
courage	*grace*	*power*
honesty	*humility*	*quality*
trust	*effectiveness*	_____
perseverance	*design*	_____

WRITE YOUR TOP TWO VALUES HERE.

WHAT DO YOU LOVE TO DO MORE THAN ANYTHING?

IF YOU WERE ASKED TO TEACH SOMETHING, WHAT WOULD IT BE?

IF YOU COULD GO ANYWHERE IN THE WORLD WHERE WOULD THAT BE AND WHY?

IF YOU HAD UNLIMITED RESOURCES, WHAT IS THE BEST GIFT YOU COULD GIVE ANYONE IN THE WORLD? (HINT, GO BIG)

WHO ARE SOME PEOPLE THAT YOU'D LIKE TO RECONNECT WITH?

WHO ARE SOME PEOPLE THAT IT'S TIME TO MOVE AWAY FROM?

WHAT IS YOUR FAVOURITE THING ABOUT YOUR WORK AND WHY?

WHAT IS YOUR DREAM JOB/BUSINESS?

WHAT WOULD YOU LIKE TO DO MORE OF?

WHAT WOULD YOU LIKE TO DO LESS OF?

IF NOTHING STOOD IN YOUR WAY, WHAT WOULD YOU DO?

PERFECT IS BORING

Feck Perfuction

— JAMES VICTORE

WHAT DOES PERFECTION MEAN TO YOU?

WHAT DOES IMPERFECTION MEAN TO YOU?

IF YOU COULD INVENT ANYTHING, WHAT WOULD IT BE?

WHAT IS YOUR FAVOURITE ASPECT OF NATURE, WHY?

DRAW A FLOWER, IMPERFECTLY.

IF YOU KNEW IMPERFECTION WAS CELEBRATED, WHAT WOULD YOU DO?

WHAT DO YOU KNOW HOW TO DO THAT NOBODY KNOWS ABOUT?

SHARE THIS WITH ONE PERSON

WHAT WOULD BE THE MOST EMBARRASSING THING TO HAPPEN TO YOU?

IMAGINE IT HAPPENED ALREADY, WHAT WOULD THAT FREE YOU UP TO DO?

USE THIS SPACE TO DRAW A SELF PORTRAIT.

WHAT CREATIVE SKILL DO YOU WISH YOU HAD?

WHAT'S STOPPING YOU FROM DOING IT?

WHAT ARE SOME SMALL STEPS YOU CAN TAKE TO START?

CONTRIBUTION HAPPENS IN THE NOW

The flower doesn't dream of the bee,
it blossoms and the bee comes.

– MARK NEPO

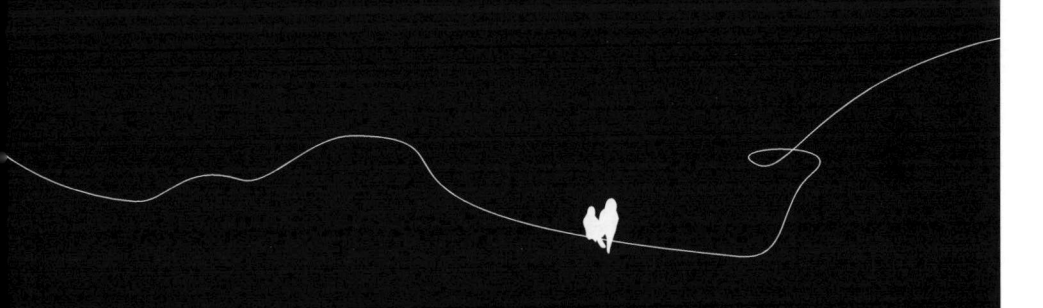

WHAT'S YOUR FAVOURITE WAY TO CONTRIBUTE TO PEOPLE?

WHAT'S YOUR FAVOURITE WAY TO BE CONTRIBUTED TO?

WHAT BRINGS YOU INTO THE PRESENT MOMENT?

WHAT TAKES YOU OUT OF THE PRESENT MOMENT?

BEING A CONTRIBUTION MEANS TO ME...

IF THERE WAS NOTHING IN YOUR WAY, WHAT'S SOMETHING YOU'D LIKE TO CHANGE IN THE WORLD - BIG OR SMALL?

WHAT WOULD THE WORLD BE LIKE AS A RESULT OF THIS CHANGE?

WHAT ARE FIVE THINGS YOU CAN DO, STARTING TODAY?

1.

2.

3.

4.

5.

WHO IS YOUR HERO AND WHY?

WHAT'S YOUR SUPERPOWER?

WHAT'S YOUR KRYPTONITE?

YOU ARE CALLED INTO ACTION, TELL THE STORY OF YOUR HEROISM!

WHAT FILLS YOUR CUP?

WHEN YOUR CUP OVERFLOWS, WHERE DOES IT SPILL OVER?

YOU ARE ALWAYS INFLUENCING

Setting an example is not the main means of influencing; it's the only means.

– ALBERT EINSTEIN

WHO HAS HAD THE BIGGEST INFLUENCE ON YOU AND WHY?

WHO DO YOU BELIEVE YOU HAVE AN INFLUENCE ON?

WHAT WOULD YOU LIKE YOUR INFLUENCE TO GUIDE THIS PERSON TOWARD?

WHAT IS THE BEST OF YOU THAT YOU OFFER OTHERS? WHAT TRAITS, QUALITY, ENERGY DO YOU BRING TO PEOPLE?

WHAT TRAITS OR QUALITIES DO YOU APPRECIATE IN OTHERS?

WHAT ARE GOOD MANNERS TO YOU?

WHAT ARE BAD MANNERS TO YOU?

WHO ARE SOME PEOPLE YOU IDOLIZE, WHY? WHAT DO THEY DO FOR OTHERS THAT YOU ADMIRE?

WHAT IS A CONTRIBUTION YOU'D LIKE TO MAKE TO YOUR COMMUNITY?

WHAT IS A CONTRIBUTION YOU'D LIKE TO MAKE TO YOUR WORLD?

WHAT IS A CONTRIBUTION YOU'D LIKE TO MAKE TO YOUR WORK?

HOW WOULD MAKING THESE CONTRIBUTIONS MAKE YOU FEEL?

IMAGINE YOU LIVED A FULL LIFE. WRITE YOUR OBITUARY FROM HOW YOU MOST WANT TO BE REMEMBERED. FEEL FREE TO EXAGGERATE AND CREATE!

WHO WOULD SPEAK AT YOUR SERVICE AND WHAT WOULD THEY SAY?

FORGIVE TO LIVE BIG

We must develop and maintain the capacity to forgive.
He who is devoid of the power to forgive
is devoid of the power to love.

- MARTIN LUTHER KING JR.

FORGIVENESS TO ME IS...

WHO HAVE YOU FORGIVEN IN THE PAST? WHY? HOW DID IT FEEL?

WHO HAS FORGIVEN YOU? WHY? HOW DID IT FEEL?

TELL THE STORY OF FORGIVENESS THAT YOU MOST WANT TO SEE IN YOUR LIFE OR IN THE WORLD?

WITHOUT OVERTHINKING, WRITE THE FIRST THING THAT COMES TO MIND UNDER EACH STATEMENT.

We are all equal

Love is my source of power

I am at home in peace

Forgiveness digests toxicity and promotes healing

I remember my innocence

I love myself enough not to accept bad behaviour

My happiness is not affected by someone else's errors

I can't be hurt, I don't take things personally

Am I willing to carry someone else's pain?

DO YOU ALLOW YOURSELF TO MAKE MISTAKES?

HAVE YOU DONE ALL THAT YOU KNOW TO DO TO RESOLVE SITUATIONS?

IS THERE SOMETHING TO DO? SOMEONE TO CALL? AN ACTION TO TAKE?

I FORGIVE MYSELF FOR...

AND NOW I FEEL...

I FORGIVE MYSELF FOR...

AND NOW I FEEL...

I FORGIVE MYSELF FOR...

AND NOW I FEEL...

I FORGIVE MYSELF FOR...

AND NOW I FEEL...

I FORGIVE _____ FOR...

AND NOW I FEEL...

I FORGIVE _____ FOR...

AND NOW I FEEL...

I FORGIVE _____ FOR...

AND NOW I FEEL...

I FORGIVE _____ FOR...

AND NOW I FEEL...

WHAT DOES THE VOICE OF YOUR INNER CRITIC SOUND LIKE?

WHAT DOES THE VOICE OF YOUR INNER CRITIC LOOK LIKE? COULD YOU MAKE A CHARACTER OF IT?

**TINY JOYS
CREATE A BIG LIFE**

Don't overlook life's small joys while
searching for the big ones.

- H. JACKSON BROWN, JR.

WHAT ARE THE TINY THINGS THAT BRING YOU JOY?

WHAT ARE THE ACTIVITIES THAT BRING YOU JOY? AND HOW DO YOU FEEL?

WHAT ARE THREE THINGS YOU DO EACH DAY THAT BRING YOU JOY?

HOW DO YOU FEEL WHEN YOU DON'T DO THESE THINGS?

TELL A STORY FROM A TIME YOU BROUGHT JOY TO SOMEONE'S LIFE

DRAW WHAT JOY FEELS TO YOU...

WHAT IS THE OPPOSITE OF JOY TO YOU?

HOW DO YOU SOURCE JOY?

WHAT IS THE GREATEST SOUND IN THE WORLD TO YOU?

WHO IS THE ONE PERSON THAT BRINGS YOU THE MOST JOY IN YOUR LIFE?

WHAT ARE TEN TINY JOYS?

1.

2.

3.

4.

5.

6.

7.

8.

9.

10.

you are
the one

JOURNAL PAGES

Date: _____

Date: _____

Date: _____

Date: _____

Date: _____

Date: _____

Date: _____

Date: _____

Date: _____

Date: _____

Date: _____

Date: _____

Date: _____

Date: _____

Date: _____

Date: _____

Date: _____

ABOUT THE AUTHOR

Erin Anderson is a Coach, Facilitator, Speaker, and Author. She grew up in Winnipeg, Manitoba, a place she credits for her love of art and culture, but when the mountains called, she answered. She moved to Whistler, British Columbia, which is where she now lives with her husband and two kids.

Erin's passion is helping people connect to their calling and commitment so they can live a big life. As the lead brand designer for the 2010 Vancouver Olympic bid, she thrived asking quality questions to get to the heart of a company's story, purpose, and brand. Through her work helping companies and individuals uncover their story and purpose in business and life, she's become a well-known transformational leader globally.

Always an entrepreneur at heart and a multi-talented spirit, Erin has led treks through the Himalayas, served as an Ambassador for lululemon athletica, owned a yoga studio, and helped many companies get clear on the "why" of their business. One thing is always consistent no matter who she's serving: Erin always contributes and impacts those around her, enabling huge shifts in their lives.

You can learn more about her coaching programs, listen to her podcast The Power to Be, or sign up for a training at www.livebigco.com

If you bring forth what is within you,
what you bring forth will save you.
If you do not bring forth what is within
you, what you do not bring forth
will destroy you.

THE GOSPEL OF THOMAS

Made in the USA
Middletown, DE
07 May 2021